TV Guide featured her on it's cover; Oprah Winfrey called her one of the "Sexiest Women In Hollywood." As the star of her own NBC prime-time show, "We've Got It Made," Teri Copley had it made. Then Jesus came, called her to leave it all and follow Him. Like Matthew of old, she left it all and followed Him.

An industry that nothing could shock, was shocked. Even Joan Rivers was shaken. On her show, she exclaimed, "Teri dear, you had so much going for you! How could you leave it all?" Someone who could understand was King David. The man after God's own heart revealed his own...and Teri's. He said, "One thing I have desired of the LORD, that I may seek after; that I may dwell in the house of the LORD all the days of my life, to behold the beauty of the LORD, and to inquire in His Temple" (Ps. 27:4).

As she dwells in the house of her LORD, as moment by moment she beholds His beauty, the more like Him she becomes.

—*Herald Bredeson*
Apostle of Faith

Teri writes in a creative way that is very prophetic, personal, and instructive. This book will inspire you to draw closer to Jesus in love and intimacy.

—*Che Ahn*
Senior Pastor, Harvest Rock Church

God reached into the pit of despair, lifted Teri up and established her feet on the solid rock of His love, grace, and truth. This book is an interesting and unique way of presenting what she is continually experiencing in her spiritual journey.

—*James Robison*
President, LIFE Outreach International

Teri has captured some of the most pressing issues of our personal growth and has presented them in a warm and non-threatening style that seizes your attention and helps explain some of the points of frustration that all of us face. It is obvious that the book has been written as a result of living through some hard things in life.

—*Dr. Scott G. Bauer*
Senior Pastor, The Church on the Way

What a beautiful story shared from a beautiful heart! Teri is the real thing, and the simplicity of the Father's love shines through her on every page of this book. You will know and love Him more after reading this.

—*Terry MacAlmon*
Popular songwriter, recording artist, and psalmist

Conversations
Between *a* Girl
and her God

Conversations Between a Girl and her God

Teri Copley

*How that by revelation He made known to me
the mystery by which...when you read, you may
understand my knowledge into the mystery of Christ.*
Ephesians 3:3

Cover design by UDG/Designworks www.udgdesignworks.com
Photography by Kaila Kuhner info@kailaphotography.com www.kailaphotography.com

Treasure House
An Imprint of
Destiny Image® Publishers, Inc.
P.O. Box 310
Shippensburg, PA 17257-0310

"For where your treasure is, there will your heart be also."
Matthew 6:21

ISBN 0-7684-3017-8

For Worldwide Distribution
Printed in the U.S.A.

This book and all other Destiny Image, Revival Press, MercyPlace, Fresh Bread, Destiny Image Fiction, and Treasure House books are available at Christian bookstores and distributors worldwide.

For a U.S. bookstore nearest you, call **1-800-722-6774**.
For more information on foreign distributors, call **717-532-3040**.
Or reach us on the Internet:
www.destinyimage.com

DEDICATION

I want to dedicate this book to my beautiful girls, Ashley and Anastasia. There is a place here on earth where you will be loved more deeply than you could have ever imagined possible, a place of innocence where you become sooo beautiful. It's a place of happiness where you can hear your heart sing. Find Him and follow Him and He will take you there! It's possible!

Love, Mommy

CONTENTS

Acknowledgments

Author Notes

Introduction

Chapter

ACKNOWLEDGMENTS

Thank you:

Delynn Buonvicino for the endless hours you've spent reading and rereading this book and working out its structure. You are a true friend.

To my sister, Julie Burns, for encouraging me to keep writing.

To all my friends whom God has used to strengthen me.

AUTHOR NOTES

One morning, as I awakened and ran to the window, pushing back the drapes to see the sun piercing through the clouds, I exclaimed, "The rain is gone; He's real. Jesus is real!" These were the happy thoughts that filled my 8-year-old little mind...

Growing up in my house, God, Jesus, church was never mentioned, and they just weren't a part of our lives. However, my neighbor—a woman named Qwen—gathered all the latchkey kids in the neighborhood and conducted a Bible study where we sang songs about Jesus. I remember tears splashing down my face as I sang about Him. I didn't know Him, and I didn't understand any thing, but I loved Him. Later on, we moved away from there.

Years passed, and the challenges of normal life took hold of my life. Success of the world embraced me as I enjoyed TV stardom, starring in a television sitcom, several made-for-television movies, and guest appearances on well known talk shows.

Then one morning while working on a movie, I woke up to a voice speaking to me saying, "Isn't the sun beautiful?" Now, as a grown woman, I did something I'd never heard of before. I knelt down on the floor and said, "Jesus, You've given me this life, and I've made a mess of it. Please take it back, and let me serve You." Suddenly a vision flooded my mind of me carrying my dead body across my arms and laying it a the feet of Jesus. Later that day, as I was walking down the street, a presence came upon me (that's the best I can describe it) and embraced me with love. I stopped dead in my tracks and cried...and this began my journey of discovering God's amazing love.

Never in my life had I considered that such love even existed, a love that filled my inner being. The emptiness and loneliness I felt were completely gone, and the pain had vanished. I thought, "Oh, my goodness, this is life!"

Then I ran into some hard times, and I didn't understand what was going on. How could we who seek Jesus hurt one another so much. How could so and so do that? And why am I so broken-hearted over what's been said by so and so? Why am I responding this way? What happened, and why does it continue to happen? You say one thing and we act another, Lord, help me!

I found my answers to these questions and others during *Conversations Between a Girl and Her God.*

INTRODUCTION

The Girl (Author Speaking)

I want to introduce you to the closest friend a girl could have. My often quiet Friend has been with me always, trying to get my attention throughout my life, but I had dismissed all of His subtle efforts to get my attention.

Then one day He woke me to the sound of His voice, saying, "Isn't the sun beautiful!" "Go home," He said. "Get your Bible, and begin reading it."

Throughout my journey with Him, He has taken away many of my fears as I've walked with Him as a person and shared love. He's held me in the night with His presence covering me. My sole desire is to see Him face to face! To be His friend!

There's only one that I do fear, and that's grieving Him. To do so is the worst feeling anyone can experience. He's so strong that sometimes I've felt I couldn't hurt Him. Yet, I've come to understand that He's also very sensitive. He doesn't get offended, just hurt. He is hurt when I hurt anyone else—even slightly. If I so much as point an accusatory finger against someone or speak harshly, then He hurts!

He gets angry as well. He does not like me to be fooled when darkness lies to me. I want to share one more thing about Him with you: He always tells me the truth. He never flatters me, as you'll see. I wish I could share with you the sound of His voice. It is the most beautiful sound you can hear. But, you will have to hear Him for yourself. I know He longs to speak to you.

There is nothing in life greater than knowing Jesus and becoming His friend. If your heart longs to know Him as your friend, be aware that it may require the greatest battle of your life. To get the greatest thing, it takes the greatest fight! Nothing in this world can be compared with Him!

Her God (God Speaking)

I would like to introduce to you my dear friend Teri. To do so, I must start at the beginning. When I formed her, I called out in perfect love, and then I "purposed" her into being. My friend is delicate in form, yet I have girded her with great strength, which she has not yet come to understand or realize. My friend has made herself known to Me, holding on to Me, choosing Me, treating Me as a friend—as a person and not a thing. I cherish that.

My friend stands firmly rooted and grounded in Me, which is where I called her and asked her to stand. She's discovered her place in My presence through overcoming many temptations and trials. The enemy tempted her to go his way by offering her the world's glory. I offered only My love and Myself. Would she choose the glory of the world or the path of obstacles?

She chose Me and wanted only to love Me and live her life as close to Me as possible. Then I called and helped her to walk out or establish her decision by stripping all of the world's glory from her. My delicate one encountered numerous obstacles placed in her path to strengthen her as I formed her into a chosen vessel of honor.

She is still in the process of becoming increasingly beautiful in My sight, and that process will continue until My purpose is fulfilled.

See, I love her with all of My heart. I see her as so much more than she sees herself, for she sometimes views herself through the eyes of man. I despise that, for I am a jealous God—jealous for her own good, to protect her! I have allowed you to see My friend without facades, open and vulnerable, to show you an example of My love performing its magnificent work in the life of one of my chosen children.

Hearing His Sweet Voice

Have you ever heard His sweet voice whisper love into your heart and soul? His Words bring healing and strength to every part of your being. Take a moment right now and listen for His wonderful voice. Pray this prayer with me:

A Prayer

Wonderful Jesus, I long to hear Your voice. Speak to my heart in a way that only You can do. Heal me of my hurts and wounds that only You really understand. Make my heart like Yours, loving, kind, generous, wise. Teach me to love You with all my heart. Amen.

Now take a minute and listen to what He says to you. Write what you hear in the space below.

_____

_____

_____

_____

_____

_____

_____

_____

_____

You are Beautiful in His Eyes

God longs to be your closest friend. And a very special old hymn says it well:

What a Friend we have in Jesus, all our sins and griefs to bear!
What a privilege to carry everything to God in prayer!
O what peace we often forfeit, O what needless pain we bear,
all because we do not carry everything to God in prayer.

Are we weak and heavy-laden, cumbered with a load of care?
Precious Savior, still our refuge, take it to the Lord in prayer.
Do thy friends despise, forsake thee? Take it to the Lord in prayer;
in His arms He'll take and shield thee, thou will find a solice there.
Charles C. Converse

He is your friend, so take a moment to listen to His voice…

The Bible says, "I've named you friends because I've let you in on everything I've heard from the Father" (John 15:15, The Message). Take a minute and get alone and quiet with God. Let Him tell you about His desire to be your closest friend. Write down what He says to you in the space provided below.

_____

_____

_____

_____

_____

CHAPTER ONE

Surrender

With surrender, love will have its perfect work.
With control, hate will have its perfect work.

The Girl

Please teach me about Your love in words that are plain enough for me to understand.

Her God

When a boy meets a girl there is much interest in things unknown. They cannot know all about the other at that first moment, but in time they will start to reveal themselves to each other. A process is birthed; it is the beginning of giving themselves to one another.

Now the process begins. First, love must be established. There will be a time of revealing what kind of love they have for each other as tests come. For when they run into circumstances and difficulties requiring hard work, their love can be proven. If the love is real, each person will labor long and hard to smooth out the difficult places. They will surrender to the testing and allow love to bloom and grow. Oh yes, the process must be nourished with plenty of faith—or shall I say faith that works through love (see Gal. 5:6).

The Girl

So…are you saying in the beginning one cannot really tell if love is real or not? Does all love look the same in the beginning, but through testing the truth of love is ultimately revealed?

Her God

Yes, do you understand? Love is a process, which means that you must walk it out. In a similar way, the longer you walk with Me the easier it will be for you to recognize, see, understand, and truly know Me.

The Girl

The process is to get me to recognize You, to know You? How does that happen? What is the process?

Her God

You will learn to know Me through a series of tests and trials, which come to reveal you to yourself. In learning who you are in My eyes, you will also begin to see and know Me. Your tests will teach you My ways and develop within you understanding. They will open your eyes in a way you've never before imagined.

The Girl

In certain respects, I think I've chosen not to see!

Her God

Yes, darkness finds its strength through deception; therefore, it works to hide you from yourself, the flesh of you! That is why I continually encourage you to open your eyes and see! See! My precious one!

The Girl

What if I fail the test and my love is proven to fall short of what You desire? What if I don't really love at all? Can that change?

Her God
Yes! I am happy to say, yes! It requires quite a few tests for a person to recognize what is in his or her heart.

The Girl
Why is that? Is it because we have lied to ourselves about what is in our hearts for so long? Are these tests a way of getting us to see what is really in our hearts? Are You saying tests are allowed for that purpose?

Her God
My greatest joy is taking an individual, and through her choices of obedience to Me, beginning a process of recreating that person back to her original structure. It involves taking her back to the way I originally created her in innocence and purity, back to the place where My love is made manifest in her.

The Girl
Your love made manifest in us? That's the part I want to know about!

Her God
I formed you, but then darkness came and made its own imprint within you. I desire for all traces of darkness to be taken away in order that you might be restored to your original purpose, to be as I originally created you. My one, this is the hard part. It is the most difficult task, so difficult in fact it happens far too seldom in far too few of my people.

The Girl

Why is all of this difficult testing so necessary. You are God! Don't You own the hearts of your people—at least the ones who have given them to You?

Her God

I own far less of the hearts of My people than they realize. That's why such tests are necessary. Most of my children do not really know what's in their own hearts! Lacking that knowledge, it becomes impossible to know truth; therefore, their understanding of the truth gets twisted.

The Girl

Wow! It seems discouraging to consider that we all must undergo so many trials. If we don't really know our own hearts, then we can't really know truth and everything gets twisted, there's so much to uncover within us and so much to have to face. It almost seems impossible.

Her God

See Hope my one! Hope is one of My best foundation stones in a person's life. It is so powerful it never gives up! (As you will see, stones represent the fruits of the spirit and rocks represent to fruits of darkness.)

The Girl

Hope believes and never gives up? Now I'm confused, because You are saying hope never gives up, but I also feel that You are telling me to surrender everything completely to You.

Her God

When you say hope, you are often referring to your desire to get things or control circumstances. My hope is for you to believe and to trust in My word.

I am teaching you to surrender your selfish desires and rights to Me so I can bring the true happiness and love that you long for. I long for you to know that love.

The Girl

Will You tell me about surrender?

Her God

The word surrender has been twisted, misused, and often misunderstood. So much has this happened that it has become a widely accepted notion that only the failed and weak know its name. In truth, resurrection power alone can speak its name and befriend it.

I am speaking of the main core of the soul. See, a person's need for control is surrender's rival. The soul is the will, the mind (thoughts), and emotions; and lives between the flesh and the Spirit of man's makeup. Most men live with the core of their soul in control, led by the enemy who establishes a foundation of fear. Control will stop at nothing to get its way, even sometimes in My name. Yet the fruit will no doubt tell its nature by the manifestation it produces.

Control gets mad when it doesn't get its way, and it retaliates by lashing out. If an individual becomes aware of its tactics, often control will attempt to disguise itself in judgment, which I despise!

Judgment has done so much damage to My children whom I dearly love. Surrender works to replace control, giving total trust to Me. When surrender is at person's core, that one takes only what is hers to have and allows My perfect timing to be fulfilled in her life. Allows, allows, allows…

The Girl

That makes me want to cry, because I understand. Sometimes our efforts to control others comes when we believe something is the truth, so we want others to believe it. Convinced we are totally right, we want them to believe it for their own good, but then we get mad if they don't believe. That's when we've become controlling.

Her God

Yes, one may have well-meaning intentions, but at the core of those intentions still is control. The person with control hidden in her heart will doubtless manifest it and alienate the very person she is trying to help.

The Girl

So, if surrender lives in the core of the soul, then all the words and intentions displayed might well be the same, but the…

Her God

...nature would be different, and, therefore, the result would be different. Do you understand? Control resides with many friends: judgment, criticism, retaliation, unforgiveness, bitterness, and hatred. Likewise, surrender lives with many friends: peace, compassion, gentleness, contentment, kindness, and love. When a heart is completely surrendered to Me then love will have its perfect work! Conversely, with control, hate will have its perfect work!

The Girl

If rocks represented the fruit of darkness and stones represented the fruit of the Holy Spirit, then surrender would be a stone. Learning to surrender is a process, right? Once surrender has replaced control, will control try to come back?

Her God

That depends completely upon each individual person. Once the stone of surrender is firmly planted inside a human heart, its foundation will manifest. The more surrender is practiced the stronger it will become until it forms a stronghold, which is very difficult to remove. Nonetheless, control will always vie to regain its place. Remember, the most crucial part is letting it sink deep into the heart and create a foundation.

The Girl

That would be the same, I suppose, for any of the rocks, right? For instance, if rock Pride is implanted and takes root through our choices, does that mean that when we act out in pride, it is practiced and roots start to grow? Then the more pride is practiced, the stronger and stronger it becomes until it's a stronghold. Does it make a foundation?

Her God

Yes, and once formed those foundations are very hard to break. Do you understand the process now?

You see, everything has a nature. Mankind tends to look at outward manifestations and react to circumstances. However, every external manifestation has an internal root in creation. My works are simple, but can be very confounding. Yet, gaining an understanding will allow love to flow freely to and through your heart.

For example a father tells his son that his shoes belong in the closet. The father has just given the son knowledge, but has left him without instructions as to how he might accomplish the task. What if the father were to say, "Son, your shoes belong in your closet. Pick them up, walk into your room, open your closet door, and put them inside." In this case, the father has imparted wisdom to his son. Now the child understands how to complete the assignment.

Beyond that the father explains his purpose: "Son, if you keep your shoes in the closet you'll be able to find them when you need them."

Now, the father gives understanding, which brings the love! Therefore, the boy feels encouraged to do the father's will. Loves encourages even the frailest souls. It hopes all things, believes all things, bears all things, and endures all things!

The Girl

God, I see something about the way You work.

God gives the knowledge: what to do. Jesus gives the wisdom: how to apply it. The Holy Spirit gives the understanding: the love to do it with.

We need the understanding part. I've experienced the knowledge and wisdom without the understanding and it feels feels like harsh judgment, which makes it difficult for me to feel love and receive what I'm being told. I just want to defend myself.

I've noticed something else. Whenever people open up to You, God, they feel You. For instance, when we sing to You, we really feel Your presence. We weep with Your love. I love feeling You!

So, now I have a really good question. How does someone get understanding? How does it come?

Her God

My one, understanding comes as a child to her father as she sits on his lap and spends time with him. You get understanding only, only, through knowing Me as I am. You must truly understand that I am a person, and together we can have a direct, intimate relationship. I draw you to Me, just as much as you are willing to come near.

As you approach, you will experience another element. Your will moves into action—your will which does not live for self but for Me.

You will immediately see the need to persevere in your attempts to draw near to Me, because all of hell will try to stop you from getting to where I am. Thus, your will moving into action will become vitally important. The Word says, "The kingdom of Heaven suffers violence, and the violent take it by force!" (Matt. 11:12). Hell will send every weapon, plan, and deceit to sidetrack, distract, and stop you, as, My one, you have already experienced.

The Girl
Yes, I have, and I still experience such things even to this day. There is so much I am not sure of. It is like walking blindly and getting hit, yet not knowing from where the punch comes.

Her God
That is only because you have so much farther to go and so much more to understand! You must continue to draw close, to know Me, and to become increasingly wise in order to not be found sleeping.

The Girl
Wait, wait! I think I know what You are going to say. To keep watch means to pray, and to be found sleeping means to be spiritual sleeping, which is not praying or being with You. Right?

Her God
To know Me is to know My Word. I always tell you that, My one. But I must say it over and over for you to know how important it is. You will not be deceived at all if you watch and read My Word! Prayer and My Word—these two are a must at all times in your life if you are to live in Me.

Developing a Surrendered Heart

Write a prayer of surrender asking God to take all of you.

_____

_____

_____

_____

_____

_____

_____

_____

_____

_____

_____

_____

_____

_____

_____

_____

_____

_____

_____

Surrender

_____

_____

_____

_____

_____

_____

_____

_____

_____

_____

_____

_____

_____

_____

_____

_____

_____

_____

_____

_____

_____

_____

_____

Do you have a foundation of control or surrender in your heart? Write about a situation that shows the "fruit" of the core of your heart.

_____

_____

_____

_____

_____

_____

_____

_____

_____

_____

_____

_____

_____

_____

_____

_____

_____

_____

_____

Surrender

Speak aloud the words to this old hymn as a prayer of consecration:

All to Jesus I surrender, all to Him I freely give. I will ever love and trust Him, in His presence daily live. All to Jesus I surrender, humbly at His feet I bow, worldly pleasures all forsaken, take me Jesus, take me now.

W. S. Weeden

God Speaks

Now give God an opportunity to speak to you regarding this matter of surrender. Write down what He tells you.

_____

_____

_____

_____

_____

_____

_____

_____

_____

_____

_____

_____

_____

_____

_____

_____

_____

_____

CHAPTER TWO

Face to Face

Mercy allows the will to choose.
Grace has made provision for the error.

Her God

What is love according to your understanding?

The Girl

I can only respond by saying what You have taught me so far, although I've been mostly unsuccessful in executing it. Perhaps I've touched on it once or twice.

Her God

My one, not only have you touched on it, but you have embraced a great depth of love. Love is the complete release of oneself to another. Now listen closely, because far too often My Words have been misinterpreted, delicately twisted, and distorted.

The key to developing a heart of love is found in losing self, as in oneself. Why? Self is the enemy of love. Self guards and protects itself. Self is full of justifications for its actions and work. But, it's root motivation is I. This, My one, is a great stumbling block for many.

Self appears to protect you, but it will block both your trust of Me and your ability to give yourself away to another. Self makes you fearful of being hurt, and reasonably so, My one. However, reason is a danger area. We must look past hurt to see into love! The expectations of man and the expectations of your own desires may leave you wounded. Come and see love! Love is trusting, free of self, and gives freely and endlessly to the needs of others. Its desire simply to be used, to give without thought of return or recognition, and definitely without "ifs." (Ifs say "I'll love you if you'll do this or I'll love you if you won't do that.")

See! My one, I am here! My love for you is unconditional love!

Selfish giving ties itself to the soul of another with an expectation of return, saying "Look what I've done for you!" Oh, the endless wounds that are attached!

My way is narrow and few find it. My love is unconditional; it needs no conditions to live. Love founded in self is human love, born of human capability. But My love heals wounds. My love is not afraid and is not offended. Perfect love is only possible when total surrender is at the core and there is complete trust in Me.

The Girl
You said I touched on it, but it is hard for me to stay there at that place of selfless love.

Her God
Love's roots are going deep into your heart. This is love that can only be formed by My power, through My Spirit, and by your choice to be near Me.

The Girl
You also said self ties itself to the soul of another. I don't understand?

Her God
That is why so many relationships are severed. One self-centered person gives to get love, but with many attachments. The other self-centered person receives to fulfill a need, but does not want the attachments. In most cases, after much strife and many wounds, there comes the severance.

The Girl

I recognize that very well from both sides. So, how does real love work?

Her God

Remember that everything has a nature. Love performs in this way: love is centered in surrender, and with surrender there are no expectations from the person to whom it's been given. It gives freely. Love, working in the receiver, is also willing to give and does not feel obligated or held by a debt.

Are you beginning to realize how love flows a river flows as its currents move in harmony?

The Girl

Yes, the undercurrents are the unspoken things we feel, and the things to which we are really responding. I think I am beginning to see. Since control is centered in self, then it is constantly working to control everything for self. Since surrender is centered in love, then it is constantly working to surrender everything to love! Right? Yes, I think I'm getting it!

Her God

Now let's move on to a more sensitive area.

The Girl

Oh, no! I hope I'm ready. I do trust You.

Her God

Listen closely to My words, My one. Love does not need to be loved! Love is loved by love. There is no need with love. Need is in the human part. As long as there remains a human longing for love, self continues to be the god. Longing or needing to be loved by man is a path filled with disappointments and wounds to the heart. I am Love in it's true nature, and only through complete trust in Me will a human heart be fulfilled.

Here is the key: have no judgment! Allow Me to take you to a high place, where fears are not hidden and weakness is not covered. It's a place where there is understanding instead of judgment and love is able to heal. It's a place where simple honesty uncovers blame, justification, and self-pity. It's a place where condemnation has no power through hateful judgments.

In My kingdom, understanding has power that's ruled by forgiveness and enthroned in love! In this place, you need not protect yourself for fear of being taken advantage of. You do not defend yourself to save face with man. In this place, you become willing to be invisible, willing to be without, willing to simply be used by God for His purposes!

The Girl

I see pride, one of self's good friends, being addressed by humility, a close friend of love.

Her God

Yes, pride is the protector of self, and humility is the sustainer of love.

The Girl
So these opposing natures, self and love, work together with powerful forces inside the heart such as pride and humility?

Her God
Yes!

The Girl
I see why relearning how to love is a process and takes time. All the friends of self are the additions that were added after the fall of man, right?

Her God
Yes, self and all its friends found their place in the human heart after mankind broke away from fellowship with God through disobedience.

Do you know what I cherish about you?

The Girl
What?

Her God
When you've encountered adversity, you've learned to choose Me and see Me instead of the evil circumstances you're in. Love doesn't see evil. How has this happened in you? During your great times of affliction, I've continually encouraged you to see Me, and now I know that My words have taken root in your heart and have transformed your very nature.

The Girl

I remember when all I saw was evil in man, and it made me not want to get too close. Now, I try to see people through Your eyes and through Your heart, and I'm not so afraid.

Her God

Evil does not abide with love, not perfect love. My one, do not be dismayed, love really can be perfected in the human heart. That is the whole purpose of the process!

The Girl

Mankind claims that we will never be perfect. But, I believe in pride we humans confuse Your perfect love.

Her God

Striving to be perfect is a weapon of pride. But, becoming perfected in love is to reflect My nature, and it is the purpose for which I formed you. Before the foundation of the world, I created you to be formed into the image of Christ, to be brought through a process.

As a child is born and grows, so we have a parallel for spiritual growth. It begins at spiritual rebirth until we stand face-to-face, which is possible right now.

The Girl

Face-to-face! I've always loved that, but I don't understand how to see You that way now. I always hear people saying that seeing You face-to-face takes place after we die and go to heaven.

Her God
Understand My Word:

> But where there are prophecies, they will cease; where there are tongues, they will be stilled; where there is knowledge, it will pass away. For we know in part and we prophesy in part. I Corinthians 13:8-9, NIV

At spiritual birth, when you believe and accept Me as Christ the Son of God, self is still god of your being. Yet, My love is imparted and rooted into your heart. Many self's friends must be replaced as I walk you through My process, which is similar to the stages of childhood development. During this process you will sometimes seem to manifest both natures.

But when perfect love has come, then that which is "in part" will be done away. "For we know in part and we prophesy in part; but when the perfect comes, the partial will be done away" (I Cor. 13:9-10, NAS).

In this process of spiritual development, the days comes to put away what is childish and walk in that which is mature. Paul said, "When I was a child, I talked like a child, I thought like a child, I reasoned like a child. When I became a man, I stopped those childish ways" (I Cor. 13:11, NCV).

My one, here is the place where most of the members of My Body remain, somewhere between birth and childhood. As you know, children are always hurting one another and touching things they should not touch. This should be a temporary, not permanent state.

"For now we see in a mirror dimly, but then face to face; now I know in part, but then I will know fully just as I have been fully known" (I Cor. 13:12, NAS). Then is when perfect love comes.

The Girl

To see You through a mirror dimly. That's while we're still children in our relationship with You. That means we see we partly through self's eyes, through our flesh, and partly through love's eyes, through our spirit. Sometimes we see You through the darkness of self, and we portray you incorrectly to others, often merely deceiving ourselves just to justify our wrong actions. No wonder the world has a difficult time believing in You.

Her God

Sadly, most see Me as being the same kind of person they are, and they portray in that way. Come, My one, and be whole and know Me. Allow My perfect love to be revealed through you.

The Girl

Is this what Your Word means when it says that we shall know You fully as we are already fully known by You? Through this process—as I die to myself, my wants, and what I consider fair treatment—I still protect self. As I learn to trust You, You then open my eyes so I can see who I really am and who You really are. When that happens will I then be perfected in love? Will I then see You through the mirror as I behold Your face through mine? If so, then I will see! I won't be blind or seeing dimly. Lord, open my blind eyes!

Her God

My one, understanding brings love!

The Girl

The process I'm going through is to get me to see You face to face, just as I will see you in heaven. But You want that to happen now while I live here on earth, not when I die.

Her God

Yes, I long for you to see Me as I am, with My perfect love completely formed in you, with My nature, My Spirit. That is the place where we will be standing face-to-face.

The Girl

One? You keep calling me One. What does that mean?

Her God

Before your birth in Me, self was your god, your spirit man was dead, and your soul was in the process of dying as your will continued to do the self's bidding. When you asked Me to become a part of you, I was birthed in your spirit; your spirit man was made as alive as it was when you were originally created. You were born again. I then began a process of healing your soul as you allowed Me. I took back possession of it through cleansing, and I took dominion over your flesh. In a sense, self was taken captive and made inactive, dead. This process completely aligned the three functions of your inner structure into unity: spirit, soul, and flesh. Spirit and soul came into agreement with the will of My Spirit in Oneness, and then in dominion over self.

You are now one in Me in complete unity of agreement, aligned in My Spirit. You are one, and I am one, and we are one together. This was My prayer to My Father for you and the rest of My body.

The Girl

Let me see if I have this right. The devil is the god of self, right? Self also works continually to take over a person's body through a process, too. Without You, the spirit man is dead and evil is free to work through the flesh (the nature of self) to possess the soul. Thus, when the spirit man is inactive through a willingness to sin, it becomes one in agreement with evil. Eventually the soul is filled with evil.

Her God

Yes, My one, completely controlled by darkness.

The Girl

Is that what happened when the first humans ate of the fruit in the Garden of Eden? Was it at that point that evil was born in man. Is that why we must be born again in You? When someone is born again of You, You enter into that person through his or her spirit man. Then through the process of cleansing You change that individual's soul. If permitted, Your spirit then rules the soul which, in turn, rules over the flesh. That person is one in perfect love, filled and possessed with You!

Her God

What joy! My heart sings because I am willing, for no one's will can be forced.

The Girl

What if a person decides not to give herself or himself to anyone?

Her God

Deception and the pride of man causes a person to think he relies only upon himself. This is satan's prideful food, deceiving him into believing that mankind needs only himself, that he is his own god.

The Girl

Most people do not understand what they are doing when they believe they don't need you, do they?

Her God

No! My children perish for lack of knowledge and are destroyed for lack of understanding (see Hos. 4:6.)

The Girl

All of this is going on and we don't know about it? Wow! Most of the time this process seems like a war, at least for me it feels that way.

Her God

It is a war over your soul, which is where your will lives.

Will you come? You hear Me say that often, don't you? Are you willing to let Me recreate you into My beautiful image, to make you one. This is My complete objective. Darkness wants to take over the will where My mercy dwells, to completely defile My creation. Mercy allows the will to choose. Grace has made provision for the error.

The Girl
You call me "My one," yet I am still divided in my heart much of the time.

Her God
I am calling you into being. I love you!

The Girl
Faith calls those things that are not as though they are! I love you!

Your Own Journey

Is God taking you on a similar path to cleansing? Are you becoming "one," united spirit, soul, and body in seeking after Him? I encourage you to step out right now and ask Him for more than you've ever before experienced.

Let me share a song I wrote during a moment of deep intimacy with Him.

I Hear You Calling

Face to face. . .I hear You calling,
Even now from this far away place.
Remove from me the deception—I hide away through fear,
And the comfort of excuses I find as I reason You away.
Even now I hear You calling,
Even now I see Your tears.

Have you ever heard Him calling you to a deeper place? Get really quiet right now and listen for His sweet voice. Write down what He tells you in the spaces below.

_____

_____

_____

_____

_____

_____

_____

_____

_____

_____

_____

_____

_____

_____

_____

_____

_____

_____

_____

_____

_____

_____

_____

_____

_____

_____

_____

_____

_____

_____

_____

_____

_____

_____

_____

_____

_____

_____

_____

_____

_____

_____

_____

_____

_____

_____

_____

_____

_____

_____

_____

CHAPTER THREE

Fervent Love

Shall you wound an already wounded man?
Wouldn't you rather accept him with grace
and allow love to work its process
to restore what's been harmed?

Her God
Do you know what a friend is?

The Girl
I think so, but I don't think I've been one, not like You.

Her God
You have tried very hard, but you've continued to have attachments, your own conditions and objectives. This is why you've experienced disappointments. I have allowed disappointment to come into your life so I can reveal unconditional love to you. See, love never seeks its own. My one, such selfless love is very difficult to obtain. In order to claim it, you must allow Me a place deep within your heart, and you must trust me very much.

In My love there is total freedom; I without expecting love in return, and I rejoice in doing of it. Mankind's love says: "If," "until," "unless." My love says, "No matter," "even though," and "forever." My love never dies; it just keeps on living.

My love endures much and counts all its sorrows as joy. It is always giving, giving, giving. There is no bottom to the well of My love. When people refuse My love then comes the hard part. It's not that My love changes, but the person who refused it cannot enter into it. To choose conditional love instead is to prefer a way of pain, for you can always fail the condition.

Rejection rules this kingdom. Rejection is a cruel friend indeed. Learn to see love's giving nature. Once you do you will no doubt cherish it as much as I. Yes, My one, Acceptance is a friend I long for you to know much more fully. With acceptance, surrender will be strengthened in your soul.

The Girl
Acceptance means to love people where they are without trying to change them.

Her God
Not by might, not by power, but by My Spirit. (See Zechariah 4:6.)

The Girl
That is the control thing again, isn't it?

Her God
Yes. Do you see why it is the core of the will?

The Girl
There are a lot of people who do things they should not. If you just accept them, it is as if you are in agreement with them. You will soon find yourself doing the same things.

Her God
We are talking about your heart towards those who do wrong—the attitudes of your heart. Not to accept them is to reject them with judgment, leaving them feeling justified in what they are doing (or have done), which has already caused them great pain. Shall you wound again an already wounded man? Wouldn't you rather accept him with grace and allow love to work its process to restore what has been harmed?

The Girl

Yes. The problem is that when they are wounded and hurt, the rejection which is ruling, hits me, and I get hurt. Then I end up responding by hurting that person with more rejection, so we both wind up in the wrong kingdom.

Her God

Yes, but I have provided a way out.

The Girl

With forgiveness through surrender?

Her God

You have said well. Be of good cheer, for love is being perfected in you. As you allow surrender to work in you, you will not be hurt by rejection. Acceptance will cover and destroy the works of rejection.

The Girl

These are coverings!!!

Her God

Yes, coverings are those things influencing your personality, those additions!

The Girl

Love covers a multitude of sins (see I Pet. 4:8). Wow! Perfect love casts out fear (see I John 4:18). Why does perfect love cast out all fear?

Her God

People are filled with many different fears. Fear allows every evil thing to paralyze or bind up an individual, stopping the flow of love in that one. Fear is very sly in its working. It hides itself by strengthening all the evils. Fear, My one, is the foundation of control.

The Girl

That's why You say to me everyday, "Trust Me! Trust Me!"

Her God

I speak those things to you to destroy the seeds that the devil has planted in your heart. What you continually hear will take root, grow, and produce.

The Girl

It seems to me the only way is to trust.

Her God

Yes, in time all come to that realization.

The Girl

What if you love those who don't want you? What if they don't want to be healed? Let's say they like things just the way they are. Then what?

Her God

If they do not want you they will leave you, but they will leave you having been loved, and it will not have been in vain. If they like things just the way they are, not wishing to be healed, and if you do not compromise your position of love and acceptance and do not judge but walk in My love, they will doubtless be convicted. Their hearts will be softened and they will desire to be healed.

Still self's covering may take over and manifest in order to protect self in them. No matter what happens, remember that love believes all things. Love is the power in the kingdom of God.

You cannot change people, you cannot force, and you cannot push. These are weapons of evil. If you try using them, they will be used against you. You must use My weapons of love to have victory. Your enemies will be disarmed and destroyed when you skillfully use my weapons of love. Do not fear, My one. Be bold in your love!

The Girl

There is so much to understand and so far to go...

Her God

Do not fear! I am faithful, so just be willing. Come, hear Me. Trust, trust, I am Spirit and I am life, and I am here to protect you. I am here to bring healing to every bit of pain in your soul, every fragment. I am here to heal the broken hearted and to set captives free. Will you allow Me? Will you open your heart? Let go of your hurt and woundedness. You do not have to prove yourself to Me. Come!

Your fear comes from the criticism residing in your mind. You see, it is in your mind and in your heart and it binds you. It is as if you are in a straightjacket, and somewhere deep down inside you know there is freedom. You want to break loose. Just let it go. You do not have to be strong; you do not have to be smart. These are things used to make you save face with the world. If you choose to save face with the world, you will lose your face with Me. Can you see? Can you see? Lose yourself. It is okay.

The world may say you are a failure. The world has its own set of standards, but they are not Mine. Mine are just opposite. My standards allow you to lose yourself. Lose the facades, the defenses, the outer clothing, the under clothing, and I will clothe you with under and outer garments and jewels and crowns and shoes. Will you allow Me? Will you trust? Will you come? Will you? Do you believe? Do you really believe?

The trials and tribulations you go through are from Me. I guide you through them because it is through these trials that the enemy is destroyed and his grasp upon your life is broken. There are many kingdoms of evil, there are many enemies, but I know the way. I won the victory. I have already conquered every single one. I know the way and I bring you through. So rejoice in the tribulation, for it is My process.

Take My hands: you can walk, you can walk. Come lame, you can walk. Your sins are forgiven. Hear my whispers in your heart. You have to be able to listen to your heart. Take notice! Hear your heart, and respond to what it is saying. What is it saying? Do you hear it? Pray for ears to hear.

The Girl

I love You. I'm tired of trying to save face. I'm weary with placing so much value on how strong or how smart I am. It's discouraging and defeating to always measure myself against others. That's walking in the pride of the flesh and its wearisome.

Is that why you sometimes allow things to be taken from us when we begin seeking our identity or strength in them? I am so grateful to You. To see You working through me is worth all that I must undergo. Your presence in my life means more to me than all the things of this world. I want so badly to be where You are! Don't ever stop moving in my life and drawing me closer to Your beautiful throne.

You say "see, see" and these thoughts keep going through my head about seeing You face-to-face and knowing You just as I am known. As long as I have known You, You have said to me, "See, see, see My one!"

Please help me to know You. No matter what, please help me to see You!

Her God

My one, you cry, yet right now you see! In this moment you see! I cry too!

The Girl

We must be willing to surrender, so I will not defend self, but put all trust in You to form us into what You want me to be. I try so hard not to be shamed by not having things or not being somebody.

Her God

If you choose to save face with the world you'll lose your face-to-face relationship with Me. Do you see? Who are you seeking to please? Just be willing to be still, so your focus is on the things of the Spirit and not on the carnal, the things of the world, where justification manufactures compromise.

The Girl

I must always be ready and willing and working to let go of self, right?

Her God

Well said.

The Girl

And compromise?

Her God

Yes, these are traps laid by evil to ensnare you through your desires—desires to have more, to be more. If you only knew how much I do have for you. Yet, darkness can pervert the heart and make it lustful and greedy, always wanting more and never being thankful for what's been given already.

Being rich is a blessing from God. Being exalted before men also is a blessing from God. I want those whom I love to be both rich and exalted, in every way. But getting there is a process that few understand or accept. Pride gets into the heart causing My process to be aborted as nursing babies choke on satan's meat, trying to live up to the criteria of being blessed.

When my people are not submitting to my beautifying process that leads to blessing they can begin to compromise as self rises up. It reaches for blessings outside of My timing, or worse, outside of My ways. After compromise comes judgment and condemnation.

But, if you see Me though your beginnings be humble, if you learn genuine gratitude and love for others, you will find that you receive all that you desire very quickly.

Let me mature, teach you, and mold you as My hands hold you. I will remove all darkness and My beautiful process will be fulfilled!

The Girl

I understand what You are saying. I believe I've been caught in this snare, and I sense that makes You unhappy.

Her God

Yes, My one. I long for you to be still and know that I am God. Be patient and listen to Me. There are many traps of the enemy to snare you. They are there to stop or delay the process of your journey with Me that takes you to where I am. See, My one, I said you are seated with Me in heavenly places. This is a process to give you understanding.

The Girl

But sometimes the journey seems so long, and at times it feels as if Your perfect plan for me will never be fulfilled.

Her God

So many distractions...so many delays. If you keep your eyes on Me the road will be straight. But when you divert your attention away from Me then life winds a very crooked road. So, be careful to keep your eyes on Me!

The Girl

I know...that's the difficult part because my mind wants to think about possessions like houses and cars—things that I desire in this life. My mind just seems to wander off.

Her God

Just focus your eyes on Me and all that your heart desires will be added to you. But, take your eyes off Me and you waste precious time.

I have formed you in My image, being three yet one, for you are flesh, soul, and spirit. I am three in one as well: the Father, Son, and Holy Spirit. The word of God became flesh, the flesh of Man, and died. I died in the flesh to destroy the flesh nature, the god of self, from where all selfish acts arise. Now I will work through you to assert that victory in your life. This happened to Jacob when he wrestled all night with me. He held on to Me through great weakness until his victory was won. This same victory must be accomplished in you, too. Do you understand?

The Girl

I think so. Because You died in the flesh, You made it possible for our flesh—our self—to die. You took its power away, but as with Jacob our flesh fights to live. We must hold on to You until our flesh surrenders to your will. When our will is submitted to Your will we change into a new person, just as you did with Jacob when his name was changed to Israel.

Her God

Unless you eat of My flesh, you have no part in Me (see John 6:56). Man ate of the fruit of the flesh, the nature of self, the god of darkness—polluting My creation! So the Word of God became flesh and dwelt among them, destroying the works of darkness! The process of which I'm speaking is all about destroying the additions—those works of darkness in the soul that add and add until the house (the individual) is destroyed...making it one in complete darkness...filled with evil.

The Girl

You came and died in the flesh destroying the flesh nature in us, removing the additions.

Her God

To make you one, in perfect agreement and harmony within your-self and with Me. In heaven, the Father, the Word and the Holy Spirit are One. On earth, the spirit, the water, and the blood agree as one (see I John 8:8). Through My death and resurrection, when My crucifixion power takes over your flesh nature by means of your dying to the desires and ways of self, then I am free to realign

you in spirit, soul, and flesh. The three parts of you harmonious-
ly agree and become as One. You are then recreated into My beautiful creation, a person led and filled by My Spirit.

Be Still and Know Me

You shall love the Lord your God with all your heart and with all your soul and with all your might. Deuteronomy 6:5 NAS

Wow! Perfect love casts out fear (see I John 4:18). Why does perfect love cast out all fear? And what are my fears that You see and I do not?

(Let the Lord speak to you and write what He says in the lines below.)

_____

_____

_____

_____

_____

_____

_____

_____

_____

_____

_____

_____

_____

_____

You must lose the facades, defenses, outer clothing, under clothing, so that He can cover you with Himself. Will you allow Him to clothe you in His love? Will you trust Him? Will you come? (Write your response to His invitation below.)

_____

_____

_____

_____

_____

_____

_____

_____

_____

_____

_____

_____

_____

_____

_____

_____

_____

_____

He wants you to take His hands so that you can learn to walk with Him in a new way. Hear His whispers in your heart. Hear your heart, and respond to what it is saying. What is it saying? Do you hear it? Pray for ears to hear.

Let this be the cry of your heart: Please help me to know You. No matter what, please help me to see You! Write to Him about how you want to meet Him and know Him more.

_____

_____

_____

_____

_____

_____

_____

_____

_____

_____

_____

_____

_____

_____

_____

_____

_____

_____

_____

_____

Yes, My one. I long for you to be still and know that I am God. Be patient and listen to Me. Just be willing to be still, so your focus is on the things of the Spirit and not on the carnal, the things of the world.

Take one hour and quietly kneel or lay still before Him, waiting for Him to speak to you. When the hour is over write about the cry of your heart, what you felt during this time, and how you feel right now.

_____

_____

_____

_____

_____

_____

_____

_____

_____

_____

_____

_____

_____

_____

_____

CHAPTER FOUR

Becoming One

Self speaks to your mind
Its desires and its deserves
Seeing everything that is not self centered
as an enemy trying to destroy it!

The Girl
Will You tell me about my soul? The soul leads most of us through our flesh, doesn't it?

Her God
Yes, My one, the soul is a slave to whomever it serves.

The Girl
Wow, so whom does my soul serve now? I need to think about that.

Her God
Your soul was made to serve your spirit. Your spirit was made to dominate your being, your spirit that is one with My Spirit in complete harmony.

The Girl
Deep down inside my heart it feels...that I miss You.

Her God
Understanding stirs up spiritual love!

The Girl
I love You!

Her God
My one, I delight in you. I say that gently, and I delight in you. Stay with Me.

Your soul, My one, is like a milky-white substance flowing through your inner person. It has doorways, entrances, and they must be guarded quite diligently because there is another substance. That one is dense in its nature, immovable in it's structure, and it longs to suck up the milky white substance. This foreigner causes blockages and paralysis, getting you stuck where you should not be.

Yet the milky substance's nature is to keep moving and will always fight to do so as long as it is able. The intruder's nature is to block the flow. That's why you get stuck. Now watch, see, and understand, My one. When you open doorways into your soul through your will, you allow the dense blackness in. Eventually it overcomes you when its is complete. Complete blockage...unmovable...not yielded...stuck.

The Girl
But what if I shut the doors and guard them?

Her God
If you ask Me, I will break up and purge all blockage. I will even warn you of dark temptations trying to enter.

The Girl
So as long as I seek You and stay close to You, I'll be okay?

Her God
Yes, but the flesh—the self of you—longs for this dense substance and despises the milky substance. Self complains to your mind, saying it is unfair that you can't have the things you desire.

Your heart and mind can be fooled into thinking that self is the real you. And it is, only it's the dead part that knows death and craves all of its nature! Self speaks to your mind continually about what it desires and believes it "deserves." It sees everything that is not self-centered as an enemy trying to destroy it! Yes! I long for you to destroy it, that you may be free, to freely flow in My love!

The Girl
I recognize what You are saying. Self protects self, and although its arguments seem right, they allow more denseness to enter.

Her God
Yes, self is a deceiver. Self works hard to appear good. But apart from Me no one is good...not one. Control is always working hard for self, protecting self.

Stay with Me! Surrender yourself to Me, and choose not to be someone in control. Watch! Allow Me to purge and purify you, for you are My precious creation.

The Girl
I must choose not to be somebody. I got that. We all want to be somebody special, huh? Then we want to make it happen and control everyone around us to help us make it happen.

Her God
Yes. Be willing to be nobody. There is a knowing I have placed in mankind, a secret place in the heart that knows and understands My love for them. Deep in that inner recess of the heart they know I've created them as someone special.

Every person feels this. Therefore, the darkness, My enemy, takes advantage and enters through pride. Pride is the strongman. It works on the person to distort, pervert, and distract him or her from My love within.

Oh, that they could see through the illusions!

The Girl

When You are saying this I hear a cry and a hurt in Your voice.

Her God

Yes, I love each one so, but there is much deception. There are counterfeits of every kind. Mankind is so deceived by self that he does not even care to know Me, his Creator. Self is god to many people.

The Girl

But some people know You, don't they? Some who know You love You, don't they? If people could see You, they would care a great deal to know You. I feel as if I know You, yet sometimes I get confused. Even in the Church people stand up and defend self. Yet, You tell me to surrender, not to defend myself. I'm sorry I get confused in this.

Her God

My One! You are not confused! You know what I have put in your spirit! Now speak it out.

The Girl
We defend ourselves and stand up for ourselves because we are still in control. Not allowing You to move us, we justify ourselves.

Her God
Go on.

The Girl
We use Your name to back up our selfish arguments, calling them Your wisdom.

Her God
What is My way?

The Girl
Your way involves allowing and trusting You to do Your will, no matter what the circumstances. You are seated at the right hand of the Father and You are over us all.

Her God
Then, My one, will you not trust Me in this?

The Girl
I want to, but I guess I'm afraid.

Her God
Of what?

The Girl
I'm afraid of appearing as a failure to other people.

Her God
Do you fear what people might say?

The Girl
Yes! I've tried hard, and they...no...I can't blame others. It's not them, it's me. I have a problem with fearing what people think and say.

Her God
Choose to stand in My ways and trust Me. If you are to see Me face-to-face, you must be willing at times to appear like a failure, and you must be willing to stand all alone. I know how difficult that can be. I paved the way!

The Girl
I know, I know. I long to know You and to be with You where You are. Please forgive me and help me. I think I'm stuck!

Where are You Stuck?

For am I now seeking the favor of men, or of God? Or am I striving to please men? If I were still trying to please men, I would not be a bond-servant of Christ. Galatians 1:10 NAS

Are you more afraid of what people think, or what God thinks about you? Ask God to reveal your heart to you in this matter. Ask Him to bring to your mind words you've said or things you've done that reveal your heart. Write about what He shows you.

_____

_____

_____

_____

_____

_____

_____

_____

_____

_____

_____

_____

_____

_____

_____

_____

_____

Does your soul look like a milky, white substance. Ask God to reveal it to you, and to reveal His Spirit within you. Now describe what He shows you.

_____

_____

_____

_____

_____

_____

_____

_____

_____

_____

_____

_____

_____

_____

_____

_____

_____

_____

_____

_____

Have you ever become stuck? Do you ever feel trapped in emotional knots and tangled in a mixture of motives—both good and bad? Talk to God about the feelings you have below.

_____

_____

_____

_____

_____

_____

_____

_____

_____

_____

_____

_____

_____

_____

_____

_____

_____

_____

Have you ever opened your will to darkness? Have you let greed, lust, anger, rage, self-pity, or any other darkness into your heart? How do these things block the free flow of God's Spirit within you?

_____

_____

_____

_____

_____

_____

_____

_____

_____

_____

_____

_____

_____

_____

_____

_____

_____

Pray this prayer of repentance:

Dear Father, forgive me for all of the ways that I've allowed darkness to enter into my heart. Forgive me for all the times I've justified that darkness within me and determined I would hold on to it. I repent for allowing blockages to come into my spirit. I repent for not allowing Your wonderful Love to freely flow through me. In Jesus name, amen.

CHAPTER FIVE

Purity

Purity sees nothing for self.
Purity sees only God.
Purity can see only Him.
All else destroys it!

The Girl

What is hidden from my sight when You say "see!"

Her God

Your eyes are often blinded to the truth of My Word and My promises. You see the natural realm; the circumstances of your life form your reality.

The Girl

I know I do. It's difficult to understand why circumstances seem to change for the worst in the physical realm after I receive a promise from You.

Her God

My one, a spiritual realm exists, and there is one who rules in the darkness part that hates you because he hates Me. This one will try to contradict everything I say. When I speak a word of promise, he works directly against it in an attempt to cause the opposite to happen. He is a defeated foe. His efforts last for but a moment, and My promise is everlasting. You, My one, will determine how long the moment of his assignment will last. Who's word will you trust?

The Girl

Yours! I trust Yours! Or should I say I try so hard to trust in Your promises, but sometimes it seems very difficult.

Her God

You have spoken correctly. Look to Me the author and finisher of your faith (see Heb. 12:2) for all the help you need. See, My one. Look to Me. I am faith. I am faith's Creator. In Me is faith; in Me is faithfulness holding you firm in the midst of disillusionment.

Truth is often veiled behind illusion. Through Me the truth is revealed. See the truth! There are deceptions of every kind masking, deceiving, and alluring through false promises of quick, instant gratification. Stand firm in Me against those lies! See them for what they are! Be willing to stand against all the allurements that come through the desires of the flesh—wanting to be, to have, to prove. See the power in surrendering, and be willing to let go so deception won't take hold of you!

The Girl

I see what You are saying. You've been telling me this for a long time. One of the most difficult experiences I have is when I think You are directing me to do something, but You are not.

Her God

My one, when this happens test your own motives—the motives of your heart. Ask yourself if you hear a voice inside your soul telling you to look at all the success others have who are going here and going there, buying this and buying that. That is the sound of the whisper of deception into your soul.

The Girl

Yes, I hear that. Can't You just make that stuff go away from my mind?

Her God
Such whispers come and go by your will and choice. I gave you a will for you to exercise it by choosing Me. Will you choose me?

The Girl
I want to; I really want to. I want more than anything be Your friend. But sometimes that's easier said than done.

Her God
Yes, My one, putting one's love into action is never easy. A woman in love responds to her husband by giving honor to him, tending to his needs, his desires. She conducts herself in a way that is most pleasing in his eyes. Yet, I am here with you, standing right beside you. But many times I am treated as an unloved husband.

The Girl
I know what You are saying is true. In the simplest form it's true.

Her God
All of Who I am is made manifest in relationship: My relationship with mankind—My relationship with you.

The Girl
Is that why I must know You?

Her God
Yes, I am a good friend, friendships require two, not just one. Your faithfulness will be revealed in time as you work through the

process of growing and developing in Me. Be patient…patient. Patience is a strong stone, an unmovable stone. Patience lives in surrender. Once patience becomes rooted in faith, it will overcome every obstacle, every storm, every wind. My one, come forward! Many of My vessels crack while patience takes root.

The Girl
Yes, yes, I know that for sure. Doubt is the enemy of patience, always working to destroy it. Isn't that right?

Her God
Yes, do you now understand? Come forward.

The Girl
Right now I love you so much. I understand; I see!

Her God
You see My process! The world may call you a failure or say that you don't know what you're doing. I say follow Me and I will show you great and mighty things.

The Girl
Wait! What about the ones who get stuck in darkness? A lot of us get stuck in various ditches.

Her God
My Word and your prayers will deliver you out of any ditch. You must prioritize, and you must fight. You must completely destroy

anything that threatens to distract your attention away from Me or to delay your progress in Me.

The Girl

Draw near to God and He will draw near to you. Resist the devil and he will flee. (See James 4:7-8.)

Her God

As you draw near to Me I will reveal Myself to you. I will teach you many things concerning Me. My promises and My Word help to draw your heart towards Me. Will you come when I call you? Will you respond as I draw you away?

The Girl

Yes! I think everyone would love to come to You, but they feel as though they can't. It's as if they are stuck in ditches. When someone is stuck in a ditch we must fight to get them out, right? Instead of just passing them by?

Her God

Many are the self-righteous who pass by, saying in their hearts, "Look where she is. She must deserve that hardship, or he's probably done something wrong and God is teaching him a lesson." The one in the ditch now begins to protect himself by becoming defensive, using self as a cover. Pretty soon self wins the battle for his soul, and he no longer yields to the power of My love that I might heal him.

The Girl

Well, many people require a lot of hard work, and some just want others to get stuck with them.

Her God

You are here to do the work I set before you. My one, as you are close to Me, My power will work for you and through you. The work will become increasingly easy. Every difficult road will become very easy if you persevere. Don't give up so soon. I am here to encourage you to do good works. You can do anything I call you to do through the power of My Spirit working in and through you. Trust Me!

The Girl

I believe what You are saying is true. What should I do about the ones who want me to get stuck with them?

Her God

It is not My will you get stuck, for getting stuck indicates an area of weakness remains in you.

It takes time and effort to know Me, not because I don't want to be found, but because of the roots of sin you must fight through. Once you say yes to sin, it's works like a weed and starts to grow. It sends out deep roots that make it strong and difficult to uproot. And weeds grow very fast. These weeds distort your sight of Me. After you let them in, you must work to get them out.

Don't be discouraged about them, for I have made a way for their removal through My Word. "The Son of God appeared for this purpose, that He might destroy the works of the devil" (I John 3:8 NAS). See! Don't be fooled!

The Girl

All works are revealed by the fruit they bare. We don't even realize it, do we? Most of what we see when we encounter these weeds is the hurt and disappointment they bring into our lives. Why do we experience so many disappointments?

Her God

My one, you are often disappointed with yourself, but I see you through another perspective. Many of the difficulties and disappointments you encounter are there to prepare you for what's ahead.

I will always show you things to come, so you will be ready. I am in one place, and you are in another. I speak of one world, you speak of another. I will always be preparing you for the place where I am. For where I am I desire for you to be also.

See! My one, see. Don't be as a blind man groping at the air, grasping at anything, trying to take hold of life. Let purity and humility lead you. Come greet these stones in My kingdom! They only live in perfect love. They can't survive anywhere else. They are very delicate and easily destroyed.

See them! Purity sees nothing for self; purity sees only Me. Purity can only see Me. All else destroys it. Will you believe Me in this? So few will, feeling justified by their own knowledge. Purity safely rests in trust. Humility is greatly mocked and despised in the heart of man, even in the hearts of My ambassadors, those who have a form of godliness it but deny its power. Few are there who seek genuine humility.

Humility, forsaking self's need to be preeminent, never holds suffering proudly as though it were a trophy selfishly obtained. No, no, I do not look at what man does. I look for a willingness to release all of self's prideful ways to Me. Where are you?

The Girl

I'm hiding in the bushes like Adam and Eve! Scared! Feeling filled with self's nature and consumed by it! You speak about a place that seems impossible to attain from where I am.

Her God

My one, I could only speak this to you if you had tasted it and seen it.

The Girl

Yes, I know. You are speaking of a place where there are no torments and the cares of this life are lost in trust. I want to go to that place of trusting everything to You, even my life!

Her God

Yes, even your life! Will you lay it down? For Me? Will you trust Me with your very life?

The Girl

I thought I had!

Her God

You have, but not completely. You are holding back some things very dear to your heart, although you don't realize it.

The Girl

I know what You are saying is true, yet I don't know what they are.

Her God

Come with Me a little farther....see the places in your heart that are snow white and pure? Yet, at times the dark soil underneath blackens it, dirtying the beautiful landscape of a peace-filled heart. Will you allow Me to dig deeply?

The Girl

Yes, how can I refuse You? I have grown to trust You.

Her God

Expose your true motives in My presence—the intents of the heart. I'm talking about the filtered, hidden, false ones. False motives wear masks painted with Christian lingo: "I mean well." "I'm just trying to be honest." "God wants us all to prosper."

You must expose the true motives of your heart, before the flesh is able to justify them and excuse them. You must actively work to lay them down.

The Girl

I have, haven't I?

Her God

Yes, but the work I speak of is even deeper, hidden far in the recesses of your heart. May I dig?

The Girl

I want to say no and fight You! But I know from doing that so many times in the past that it only makes the process worse. Please dig gently.

Her God

I dig so gently that it often goes unnoticed. My one, My nature must be formed in you to fully fulfill My Word to you. Once that happens, all else shall be added unto you.

The Girl

The things You add, are those the promotions, blessings, promises? I think most of us want the things added first.

Her God

Yes, and if I did that self would gladly pervert them, and pride would ruin the wonderful masterpiece I'm creating in your heart. Allow Me time to form you. I will keep the things to be added safely for you until you are ready for them. Trust Me, My one.

Precious Promises

I come to the garden alone,
while the dew is still on the roses;
and the voice I hear,
falling on my ear, the Son of God discloses.
And He walks with me, and He talks with me,
and He tells me I am His own,
And the joy we share as we tarry there,
none other has ever known.
C. Austin Miles, 1868-1946

He wants to draw you nearer today in order to reveal Himself to you. There in His sweet presence He will reveal Himself to you. Will you go? Write what your heart is saying to Him in response to His drawing.

_____

_____

_____

_____

_____

_____

_____

_____

_____

There in His holy presence He will give you promises, precious promises of His work of wholeness and love. Ask Him to give you His promises. Write out your request as a prayer.

_____

_____

_____

_____

_____

_____

_____

_____

_____

_____

_____

_____

_____

_____

_____

_____

_____

_____

_____

_____

_____

_____

Draw me, we will run after thee. Song of Solomon 1:4

Will you come when I call you? Will you respond as I draw you away? How will you answer His love? Will you wait quietly in the stillness of His presence in order to learn about His love? (Write your answer below.)

_____

_____

_____

_____

_____

_____

_____

_____

_____

_____

_____

_____

_____

_____

_____

_____

_____

_____

_____

Purity

Alone in His wonderful presence, write the promises He gives you.

_____

_____

_____

_____

_____

_____

_____

_____

_____

_____

_____

_____

_____

_____

_____

_____

_____

_____

_____

It's difficult to understand why circumstances seem to change for the worst after you receive a promise from God. Describe when this has happened to you in the past.

_____

_____

_____

_____

_____

_____

_____

_____

_____

_____

_____

_____

_____

_____

_____

_____

_____

_____

_____

_____

In the past, has the enemy of your soul ever been able to steal away that promise when you truly embraced it with faith and love? Do you believe that God will keep His promises safe from the enemy's hands?

_____

_____

_____

_____

_____

_____

_____

_____

_____

_____

_____

_____

_____

_____

_____

_____

_____

_____

Why does the enemy want to steal your promises from God?

_____

_____

_____

_____

_____

_____

_____

_____

_____

_____

_____

_____

_____

_____

_____

A Prayer for Your Promises

Dear wonderful Father, hold my promises in the palms of Your loving hands. Keep my heart in Your loving embrace. Surround my life with Your Spirit, and comfort my soul with Your sweet, precious love. Draw me often, and speak to me always. I love You forever!

CHAPTER SIX

Unconditional Love

*Coverings of hate, hating you,
causing you to hate.
Coverings of love, loving you,
causing you to love...*

Her God

My one, do you believe? Do you really believe? If so, stand! Stand with Me in faith. You must first believe I am a real person, not an entity to hold away at a distance, but your best friend.

Stand against all you see, against all you hear. To stand in faith doesn't mean to hope that something may happen. Standing in faith involves knowing it will occur, because I was the one who spoke it. I made the promise and cannot lie. Believing...to believe is not to hope but to know. Believing takes faith.

The hope I give is an anchor for your soul, and is entirely different than the hope you wish for. Worldly hope is empty, useless longing...striving. Hope in Me means trusting. It is a trust that secures faith. Hope secures, hope trusts Me that I am real, that I am here, that I am God!

The Girl

I love that! That's why you subjected the whole creation to futility, because You subjected it in hope. Your Word says, "The creation was subjected to futility, not of its own will, but because of Him who subjected it, in hope..." (Rom. 8:20 NAS). You chose to trust us to choose You.

Her God

Choosing...willing...You are allowing Me to simply transform you into My beautiful creation, to unite you to Me so that we may become one, standing face-to-face! You please Me so when you trust Me, when you believe Me!

The girl

Tell me more about hope, will You? I have a hard time understanding that one.

Her God

Trust and hope, without either one of these you shall stumble and fall.

The Girl

Yes! I remember when I saw You in a vision sitting next to me and you taught me that? You had three stones in front of You. You asked me, "Which of these do you think is the most powerful?" Suddenly, I said, "The one I throw the farthest."

You answered, "You've said well."

I then threw each one of the stones. Then You said "Now this is faith, this is hope, and this is love. If you don't throw them they become a stumbling stone. Hope is trust."

Her God

The anchor of your soul is found in trusting Me. Faith moves on hope! Faith takes action to hope! Love covers.

The Girl

Oh wow! Faith acts out the hope, and love covers everything, right?

Her God

Yes, or hate, its rival, will cover if you are in doubt! Doubt doesn't move. Fear paralyzes it. Hope releases faith!

The Girl

I think I'm really starting to understand Your ways a little better, and it's helping me to believe in You even more.

Her God

Hope knows deep inside that faith is possible in every situation! If hope doesn't know, faith won't move!

The Girl

Yes, yes, hope knows, without a doubt, and moves faith! How does hope know?

Her God

I speak! I am hope. Stay with Me, knowing Me. I am a person; I am a friend. When you spend time with Me, you become My friend and I tell you all about Me. I share My heart, My plans, My will.

The Girl

And darkness tries in every way to stop that from happening!

Her God

You are beginning to understand!

The Girl

Understanding through experiencing something brings love. For example, when I've been ill I feel more compassion for others who are ill. That experience has brought love. Is that correct?

Her God

Remember I told you you'd suffer many things for Me?

The Girl

Yes, I sensed Your presence so powerfully, but it was difficult to think about suffering. Yet, Your presence was so wonderful, comforting, and loving that I said "Gladly Lord! I'd do anything for You."

Her God

Yes, to die to self is painful. All selfish desires and facades must go. It's a price that you must pay to know Me intimately.

The Girl

It's very hard. I'm so glad it's a process, and that I have time to learn and grow in it. I think I'm even beginning to like and honor the process, because I see what it produces.

Her God

It produces intimacy, oneness, with Me.

The Girl

There is nothing, nothing that compares to knowing You!

Her God

My one, I love you! Once more I'm calling you into being! In the stillness of your soul, see the trust as you wait on Me. Don't be moved by the conditions around you, the what ifs and maybes.

Come to Me! See? You must come, for it's an action you must do. I have waited for you to come to Me, to where I am, through prayer communication with Me. Your personality and My personality are communing with one another. I love you.

Begin to understand My likes and dislikes. Know Me as I am; create an atmosphere for Me, as I did and continue to do for you. Did I not say I go to prepare a mansion for you?

Relationship, friendship. These things are very important. Equally important is not hurting the ones I love in My body, not spitefully speaking in coarse jesting, as if I can't hear you, as if I've disappeared. I have no where to go, I am ever present. Remember, I'm your friend and I love you!

The Girl
My life is filled with distractions. With all the noise and the things we have to do, it's so easy to forget You are here.

Her God
Yes, business, business. Going about accomplishing all that business. But...Mary, Mary, where is the Mary who will sit at My feet and enjoy My presence? (See Luke 10:39,41.)

The Girl
I hear You!

Her God
I would call for her. I am calling for her to come into My presence, and at her weeping I would weep! Her love and devotion would stir my heart to do the miraculous.

The Girl
Mary represents that one who will be still, worship You, see You, hear You, and know You!

Her God
Later when Martha came to me, even though she made bold confessions of faith, I didn't move from where I was. I asked her to go and get Mary. Then when I saw Mary weeping I wept and was moved to raise the dead. Mary, Mary, who is this Mary? Where can I find this heart today?

The Girl
To You! They followed her to where You where and to where You did the miraculous! (See John 11:24-44.)

Her God
Why didn't I move on Martha's confession of faith? Why did I call for Mary?

The Girl
Because she was Your friend. There was intimacy and oneness between You.

Her God
She was My friend!

The Girl

Oh, to be Your friend, to be a friend of God! You are my friend, but I want to be Your friend! That's the fellowship that was broken by sin in the garden! You know what thought just struck me? You miss us! Do You miss us?

Her God

Broken trust, broken friendship...My heart yearns for friendship with mankind. I created my people with so much love intending for them to fellowship with everyday, in complete trust with Me.

The Girl

We broke that trust through our own will.

Her God

Sin created a great, wide gulf between us. The serpent deceived and brought separation and death, but now there's a way back to Me. I came in the flesh to bring reconciliation. I came in the same form that was deceived to bring truth. I am a God of honor. I long to regain My fellowship with you.

The Girl

Friendship, friendship. Sometimes it's hard to be a good friend to people we physically see, and most people aren't even a friend to themselves.

Her God
If hate is in you it will hate you. If love is in you it will love you. Whatever is in you will be unto you.

The Girl
Darkness and self's coverings work against us?

Her God
Despising you while causing you to despise others.

The Girl
I know that is true. Coverings of hate, hating us, causing us to hate.

Her God
Coverings of love, loving you, causing you to love.

The Girl
I'm going to need all of Your coverings to be Your friend because I always fall, or fall short.

Her God
Yes! A child learning to walk has great difficulty at first, and falls a lot, but the parents rejoice in his trying, and celebrate over the few steps taken.

The Girl
Is that what You do? You look at the good we do?

Her God
Strengthening you in your weakness. I want you to be My friend!

The Girl
I believe You are about to have a lot of new friends. I believe people want to be Your friend.

Her God
Many are weighed in the balances and left wanting. They don't have time to be My friend.

The Girl
But if I know You, You will use the ones who are Your friends to demonstrate friendship with You, so others might SEE You!

Her God
So you know Me?

The Girl
A little, I do.

Her God
I'm calling you into being, My friend! I love you.

Three Stones

Faith, hope, and love are three stones that form a foundation of your walk with God. Have you ever thought about these three qualities of the heart? If you choose to allow God to develop them in your heart, write a prayer making that request.

_____

_____

_____

_____

_____

_____

_____

_____

_____

_____

_____

_____

_____

_____

_____

_____

_____

_____

Do you choose to believe, to really believe? Get quiet before God and ask Him to show you faith and hope for your own understanding. What did He reveal to you? Record it below.

_____

_____

_____

_____

_____

_____

_____

_____

_____

_____

_____

_____

_____

_____

_____

_____

_____

_____

_____

_____

Understanding coupled with experience brings love. Describe how this has happened in your life.

_____

_____

_____

_____

_____

_____

_____

_____

_____

_____

_____

_____

_____

_____

_____

_____

_____

_____

_____

_____

If Jesus sat down beside you and asked you to be willing to suffer many things for Him, what would be your response? Write it below.

_____

_____

_____

_____

_____

_____

_____

_____

_____

_____

_____

_____

_____

_____

_____

_____

_____

_____

He is calling you to come deeper into the stillness of prayer. Wait before Him until you sense His sweet presence. Then write what He speaks to you. Come!

_____

_____

_____

_____

_____

_____

_____

_____

_____

_____

_____

_____

_____

_____

_____

_____

_____

_____

_____

_____

_____

_____

_____

_____

_____

_____

_____

_____

_____

_____

_____

_____

_____

_____

_____

_____

_____

_____

CHAPTER SEVEN

Inside the Heart

I hear You cry in my heart, "come"
Please tell me why I am not in the place you speak of
The place I see in my heart
This place of perfect love?

The Girl

How will I know the difference between my own voice, a voice from darkness, and Your voice speaking to me?

Her God

My one, My voice is first peaceful, and lives in My nature of love. My voice speaks My Word, and never speaks contrary to it.

The Girl

But sometimes we think we hear Your voice, even in those vague areas that are not directly related to Your Word. Sometimes we think we are doing the right thing, yet it's wrong. I've been wrong.

Her God

My one, listen carefully to the motives of your heart. Listen carefully to the fruit of your lips and the thoughts of your heart. Do not allow reasoning and justification to rule! My one, hear truth from the heart, for out of the heart the mouth speaks (see Matt. 15:18). Man can fool himself with many justifications, and justifications are a lie. The root of justification is a lying spirit.

My one, listen to your heart! See My way in truth, for you shall know the truth and the truth will make you free! Whom are you aiming to please? See the struggle of man. Man is a master at pleasure, self-seeking, and pursuing his own gain. My one, do not go the way of Cain, who for the selfishness of compromise was not rewarded as he supposed he would be. Rather, he was deceived and opened his heart up to hatred and murder. He brought in the ultimate fruit of destruction through jealously of another, rooted in his own failure. What loss!

The Girl

Cain was working very hard in his own strength to please You. When we work so hard in our own strength to please You, we put value in our ability and then fall into a pit of self-righteousness and pride. And when we are not rewarded as we imagine, we become very angry and hurt. I have been there, haven't I?

Her God

Yes, My one, and there is so much more in this area I long to teach you. For now, let us continue speaking about the ways of your heart. Bring your broken heart to me, your heart longing just to be heard, crying with despair and desperation. My one, bring all brokenness and entrust it to Me. Remember My Word. I am God, and I am here with you, and I am with those who call on Me.

The Girl

A broken heart? Needing to be heard? I recognize that.

Her God

Yes, you do, all too well. You've suffered years of brokenness, being broken again and again. My one, the expectations of man creates your disappointments. Accept others to who they are, and stop trying to change them in your own mind. Your own expectations will not be met, and satan delights in seeing the hurt you feel when that happens. My one, release all your expectations to Me, for I will never disappoint you.

The Girl

Yes, Lord, I get stuck here all the time. Why do I continue to get stuck here?

Her God

The biggest reason is human love—conditional love—the need to be loved and accepted by man. Remember when I spoke earlier of the need to be loved? My one, you are loved! Eternally loved, beyond measure, and no one can take it from you!

The Girl

OK, You brought up a very sensitive issue for me, this human love from a man. All my life I have longed for this love from a man who would cherish me and be so proud of me.

Her God

I am the rib for your comfort and protection. Rest in Me! I love you.

The Girl

Sometimes it's even hard for me to believe You love me, because mostly I've known critical love.

Her God

My one, believe in Me, and trust in Me! Do not hold to the words of man, who through their interpretation of Me claim to be so wise, yet are so very, very, foolish. Do not hold on to your own life and a desire to be known by all. My one, all of heaven knows your name. Be willing to forsake all and follow Me. Come closer! The subtleties of satan twist and distort the truth, using self-righteousness reasoning of to pervert My way. My one, see truth and understand.

The Girl

It seems so complicated and muddled.

Her God

Yes, many are unable to see. Come to the clear waters of purity through humility, and never become self-righteous. Always examine yourself, testing all your thoughts and motives by My written Word. Speak the truth in love, purifying the waters of this well inside of you, so that all may see clearly through you. Do not allow anything to remain hidden. Expose to Me all you keep in secret, confessing your weaknesses so they may become your great strengths. This is how My Word is made manifest in My people whom I love!

The Girl

Your Word made manifest? I think I'm beginning to understand something here. Your Word is made manifest by something we do, when we act in faith. Your Word is alive, and when we act on it we see come to life. It is living truth!

Her God

Well said. To believe in something is to act on it. One goes with the other, which is why faith without works is dead (see James 2:26).

Without the action of works, there simply is no faith. Simple truth! Do you believe? Do you really believe?

The Girl

In some areas I do and some not so much I guess. I'd like to have faith in all areas of my life.

Her God

You have spoken truthfully, not comparing yourself with others, but facing where you are and allowing Me to strenghen and heal you. You are experiencing freedom in Christ, where condemnation has no voice! Stand, My one, I am here!

The Girl

Tell me what it is that makes man prone to so much weakness, to so much sin, which brings so much reproach to You.

Her God

My one, as you know and understand how the flesh craves to have. The lusting of the flesh is to obtain. This is the seed of satan.

The Girl

The flesh has feelings? It also thinks?

Her God

Not only does it think, but it connives and schemes as a sly serpent lying in wait as it plans an attack. As a serpent is quick, similarly deception quickly gets covered by good intentions and goes unnoticed. You see? The will believes a lie, then it has its own way. This often happens in My people.

The Girl
Let me be sure that I understand You. The flesh sees what it wants and then plots the best way to get it, quickly covering itself with good intentions. This really is deception, the plan of the cunning serpent. The flesh goes in for the kill, willing and ready to destroy all that gets in its way.

Her God
Yes, destruction is its fruit.

The Girl
That's scary, but I understand. How do we who are Your people and confess You in our lives change these things? How do I change?

Her God
I teach you as you are willing, because only a willing heart learns and trusts and receives. Change can be a painful process. The flesh cannot be improved, but must be destroyed completely at every turn, with every choice so that your new nature can live. You see, all the flesh is and all that it tells you is a lie, counterfeiting everything I've promised, creating many distractions.

Deception seeks to lure you down the wrong roads. It dangles a carrot saying, "This is the way, walk in it." But, its end is destruction. Keep your eyes off the blessings you want, and keep them on Me and great will be your reward. Hear wisdom's voice calling at every corner, with prudence by her side. Follow her paths and see her end.

The Girl

Lord, I'm not that smart. Help me, Lord, to understand.

Her God

Do not listen to the wisdom of man, the mindset of man, which protects self and honors self with self-righteousness at its side. No! Remember Peter's mistake when he said: "Far be it from You Lord, this shall not happen to You" (see Matt. 16:22-23). The wisdom I speak of here is the wisdom of the Spirit. Hear the Spirit.

The Girl

The mindset of man wants the flesh to live and be strong.

Her God

Yes, My one, and it must die. The flesh must be utterly destroyed. Then the real you shall live.

The Girl

You say it must be done, and I think You are talking about this happening now while we are living on earth. Otherwise, why bother, right?

Her God

Yes, My one, while you are alive on earth.

The Girl

Why do so many say that this will happen only after we die?

Her God

It is an excuse, a justification disguised as knowledge. The flesh's mind is filled with self-protection, which is sends to your will and thoughts. It can live in you like a parasite, and you just think it's you. The flesh becomes intertwined in the soul, and takes dominion over the spirit. Learn to recognize the voice of the flesh when it says, "Me, me me; what is right for me; what is fair for me."

The Girl

These statements about what is right and what is fair are provoked through the hurt inflicted by others.

Her God

Yes, and the cycle continues on and on. Excuses and blaming others are lies. Bad fruit is a bad fruit, and good fruit is good fruit. Why allow justification and excuses to confuse you—to cover you? Remove the veil. It was torn for you. Remember My death, My one. The fruit of the Spirit is love. It is made known by peace, joy, gentleness, longsuffering, and self control. Surrender your will to these and give no place for the flesh and no opportunity to satan. Give him no place in your mind. Doing so hardens your heart, the place where compassion lives.

The Girl

My heart carries my emotions?

Her God

Everything goes through your heart. Remember I said that from your heart will flow rivers of living waters (see John 7:38), and from the abundance of the heart the mouth will speak" (see Matt. 12:34) It also says that it's from the heart that evil thoughts and adulteries, fornications, murders and such proceed (see Matt. 15:9).

Therefore, listen to your heart. Does your heart speak the flesh's thoughts, the mind of man? If so, repent! Be willing to acknowledge those thoughts to Me, and I will strengthen you in My power and love. The fruit of My Spirit inside you will destroy the flesh nature in you.

The Girl

Isaiah says, "Is this not the fast I choose...not to hide yourself from your own flesh?" (Isa. 58:5,7 NAS) When I read that it stood out. You promise the flesh can die?

Her God

It is the purpose of My cross! Yes, every day as you choose to surrender self to Me My nature gets stronger and stronger. Do not fear, for as you take one step at time it becomes easier and easier. There is a place of rest in Me where walking by My Spirit becomes very easy.

The Girl

More of You and less of me. That's a place where "it is no longer I who lives, but Christ lives in me" (Gal. 2:20 NAS). A place of rest? No more condemnation, hurt, or fear?

Her God

Yes! When My process in you is complete and My purposes are fulfilled you will then see Me face-to-face. You will see Me as I am, in you and through you. Your face will shine with My presence. See Me behind the veil, as My glory covers you. This is My heart's cry!

The Girl

And my heart cries too! I hear Your cry in my heart! Please tell me why I am not in the place I see in my heart, this place of perfect love.

Her God

My one, I love! The one whose heart is entwined with Mine! The one who leans on My bosom as I hold her so near! Yet, there is a timing! It is in My perfect timing that I walk you through the process to understand and experience and strengthen you for what is ahead.

My one, see My way as I take you through natural circumstances to restore My nature in you and dispose of all the false images of self.

Listen to your heart. Where is your heart? "For where your heart is there your treasure is also." Where is your heart? Surrender all things to me. Your heart treasures will change! Focus your heart on others for My Name's sake.

The Girl

Lord, help me! If I forget Your commands I so easily go back to self.

Her God

If you love Me keep My commands. I kept My Father's commands. I love My Father, and by His command I went to the cross. I believed in My Father.

The Girl

By commandment You went to the cross. You said I must take up my cross and follow You. I must do it. I must believe, really believe in You.

Her God

Yes, My one. To fully trust Me makes you able to lay down your life and to die to yourself, surrendering to Me, yielding all you are and do to Me—especially what you do and expect from others. Yes, and even what you expect from Me. Faith believes with longsuffering by its side. Surrender brings joy until My timing is complete.

The Girl

I want nothing of my own. I choose to own nothing of myself. I give everything to You. I want You to be my everything.

Her God

Whole and complete. One will carry you. My daughter, allow My purpose and love to have full glory! I love you.

The Girl

That's Your purpose, isn't it—for me to see You face-to-face through the eyes of perfect love. I have felt the freedom in complete servanthood to You. Just a glimpse of it. There was nothing of Myself I wanted. I was content in Your love and Spirit. The only thing I possessed was love, the innocence of life, the beauty of Your creation.

Her God

This love only comes when you surrender all of your desires. When you think nothing of yourself, but rather consider others. My one, love is power! The power to overcome evil. Do you see?

The Girl

Yes, I see. In this moment I see. Yet when I get hurt I only think of myself. When will it change?

Her God

When you get hurt, you respond to protect yourself. I am here to protect you as you trust Me with yourself. My one, you come crying to Me over and over to be delivered from your adversary and yet I have already defeated him. I have empowered you with love and authority in the Spirit. Now watch as you take spiritual authority in the spirit realm while in the natural you love your enemies and those who persecute you. These two, working together, destroy the works of darkness. My one, I am always here to rebuke the storm. Faith says to believe in what I have given you and act on it. Trusting and believing in Me.

The Girl

Why don't I do it? What's hindering me in that moment?

Her God

You must let go of self and abandon pride. I am humble and meek.

The Girl

Oh Lord, help me. I know what you are saying is true, yet I often get stuck. I do believe in You!

Her God

I believe in you!

The Girl

I must make this choice in this moment, right? I will to do it Your way, so help me to choose Your way.

Her God

Defending self is much less painful than being afflicted and not opening your mouth.

The Girl

"As a lamb to slaughter?"

Her God

Yes, My one, for death is swallowed up in life!

The Girl

Life comes through sacrifice of the flesh.

Her God

Come, let us journey further. See the faith building I'm erecting inside of you? See its strong foundation? The walls are secured and tight? Beams hold those walls, and they keep it erect through the storms and trials of life. See the roof, My one, every shingle brought on by obedience, which protects from turbulent storms.

The Girl

Obedience covers the house where the glory is. The glory keeps the great storms out?

Her God

My one, obedience to My Spirit will secure you. Total surrender and obedience leads to the completion of the structure!

The Girl

Obedience!

Her God

Come and let us build here!

The Voice of God

Have you ever asked God, "How will I know the difference between my own voice, a voice from darkness, and Your voice speaking to me?" Ask Him to explain, and write what He says to you.

_____

_____

_____

_____

_____

_____

_____

_____

_____

_____

_____

_____

_____

_____

_____

_____

_____

_____

Do you seek the love of a man? Can you lay down even this love before the Father. Doing so allows the Father to love you through that person, and you will become free to give His love into the relationship. Write out a prayer asking God to take you to this whole new level in your human love relationship.

_____

_____

_____

_____

_____

_____

_____

_____

_____

_____

_____

_____

_____

_____

_____

_____

But we all, with open face beholding as in a glass the glory of the Lord, are changed into the same image from glory to glory, even as by the Spirit of the Lord. 2 Corinthians 3:18

Many are unable to see Christ within them. He is calling you to come to the clear waters of purity, through humility, never becoming self-righteous. Examine yourself and tell Him about impure ways that may be hindering you from coming into His presence. No secret sin is hidden from Him. Repent for every one.

_____

_____

_____

_____

_____

_____

_____

_____

_____

_____

_____

_____

_____

_____

Take a moment and get very still before Him. Listen to His voice speaking into your heart. What is He telling you about the sin you just confessed to Him?

_____

_____

_____

_____

_____

_____

_____

How do you see the flesh wanting to live and take over, instead of dying in you? Do you want this selfish nature to be killed. If so, tell the Lord about it in the lines provided.

_____

_____

_____

_____

_____

_____

_____

_____

Have you ever taken time to listen to your own heart? Listen to it right now. What is it saying? Does your heart speak the flesh's thoughts, the mind of man? Repent! If so, ask God to change your heart so it speaks His thoughts. Write down what your heart is saying.

_____

_____

_____

_____

_____

_____

_____

_____

Do you want all of Him and nothing of yourself? If so, write a prayer of consecration.

_____

_____

_____

_____

_____

_____

_____

_____

If you need Him to help you to make this decision, tell Him that.
Write down what He says about your prayer of consecration.

_____

_____

_____

_____

_____

_____

_____

_____

_____

_____

_____

_____

_____

_____

_____

_____

_____

_____

_____

Oh! It is good to soar
These bold and bars above,
To Him whose purpose I adore,
Whose providence I love;
And in thy mighty will to find
The joy, the freedom of the mind.
Madame Jeanne Guyon

CHAPTER EIGHT

The Cross

I saw the resurrection
The resurrection I put before Me
And the love of My Father

The Girl

What is hidden in the heart? Are the undercurrents of all the manifestations of the fruit we bear hidden deep in there? The heart is where shame hides.

Her God

Yes, My one, understanding is taking root. I suffered shame painfully. My clothes were torn from My body, and I hung naked before many people as they mocked, slandered, and ridiculed Me. It was the price of shame, so that you live free of it.

Free from shame, you can live in the beauty of nakedness (innocence), which is created in purity.

The Girl

Yes, I am seeing something I've never seen before, and it makes me want to cry.

Her God

Do not inflict this pain on others, My one. Be sensitive to the nakedness of man's heart as he reveals himself and comes out from those bushes to face truth. I covered my people with new flesh—the flesh of the Son of Man. It's My way.

The Girl

When shame came, Adam and Eve tried to cover themselves with fig leaves, just as we try to cover and protect ourselves. Yet, You covered them with flesh skins, revealing the flesh of Jesus that would cover us.

Her God

Yes, the depth of the fall of mankind was very great. There's a process of understanding that must come before restoration. Man and woman became so completely blind, deaf, and ignorant that at first I could only speak to them through outward, natural circumstances. It was a way to lead them to see and understand the inward, the spiritual.

The Girl

That's why You brought the Law, to reveal to us where we were and show us the depth of our darkness? You know what? I bet when Eve didn't immediately die physically after eating the apple that she might have wondered if you lied, not realizing she was taking the road to death.

Her God

This is true. Yet, Eve knew she had died spiritually in that instant. She knew she had drastically changed. Fear and shame did cover her immediately.

The Girl

Fear is the most horrible feeling ever! But wait, just as you suffered shame to clothe us from it, you also experienced fear in the garden as You sweat great drops of blood.

Her God
Yes, My one, all of what I experienced provided a cover for man and woman, a way to come back to Me. I took sin in all its fullness for you, so that you, My one, would be free in Me.

The Girl
That's the resurrection? You came to the disciples in the flesh to show them new life in human form. It's available right now, not just when we go to heaven.

Her God
When you believe in Me and trust in Me you are free to live in the resurrected life.

The Girl
I understand that! What did You do with all that hurt?

Her God
I saw the resurrection! The resurrection was always before Me! And the love of My Father!

The Girl
The love of the Father was poured out through You…to us!

Her God
I love you! Come with Me farther…In My kingdom, in My life, where there is no death. My one, there is only love. As I

love and as My love is poured out through my vessels, then the world sees Me!

There are many bound in deception who cannot see the truth. Mercy allows you to see truth for them.

The Girl

And when my motives are pure and only love lives in me, I speak the truth to them with understanding, so they might see?

Her God

Yes, it's My way! It's My kingdom come to earth, My will done on earth as it is in heaven!

The Girl

I know You cry for us to love each other! I remember the vision You showed me of You overlooking Your people, and one of them lightly slapped another on the cheek. How you grieved over that. I hear your heart cry over the sheep killing the sheep, and how You want us just to love each other. But, My Lord, we don't really know how to truly love because we are confused. We are mixed up with so much wisdom of man. Our understanding of love is mostly based on self, and we believe it is Your love. We are terribly deceived.

Her God

Sadly, it is as you say, My one. Yet My love is about to be poured out as never before to My people, for My mercy's sake.

The Girl

Lord, will you help us to love You? To know You?

Her God

Unless you abide in Me you become desensitized, dulled in your ability to feel My presence and My life. As My love is poured out over those who receive Me, the darkness will counteract My grace with selfishness and deception and the love of many will grow cold.

Many are the Pharisees in My body whose life is in their flesh. They glory in themselves. Even so, they think it is for Me!

See the love of a tender heart, feel its beat! A cry of despair sounds all around the world, seeking and wanting My love, searching to find only what is found in Me. Love!

My one, see the difference! Some of My people walk in selfish ambition, envy, slander, judgment, criticism, and hatred. They claim to be wise, but they are not.

The Girl

Pharisees in the church? My Lord, are You saying the man of the flesh, the carnal man in the church, is a Pharisee?

Her God

Yes. Deception is a lie hidden and mixed with some truth. A time is coming when I will only pour out My anointing through those vessels who have completely died to self. Humble yourself in the smallness of things, for here is the power of life.

The Girl

Little things become big things, right? Little steps become great big steps. It's all how we see things, what we see is what we understand.

It's so hard to cling to the cross when it's time to die to self. Do You know what I mean?

Her God

Yes, of course I do, My one. I delight in you.

The Girl

Yes, Lord. In prayer, through visions, You have been revealing Your cross to me. This is what I have seen: All of sin in its entirety, all that ever was and will be came upon You.

Your blood was shed.

The scourging of Your back, the thunderous sound of pride of mankind being broken, as they stood believing he was right. With power they beat You as You fell to the ground under the strokes of the whip.

Your blood was shed.

You experienced the rejection of those you loved and kept so near: Peter and the rest. They praised You one minute and denied You the next. You experienced the battle of the mind, the fullness of satan's attacks against your thoughts as they crowned You with the crown of thorns.

Your blood was shed.

Your hands were nailed down to the wood, pierced for the works of men who glory in themselves.

Your blood was shed.

Your feet were nailed down for the paths we choose, for our own desire. Your blood was shed.

The spear pierced Your side, which symbolized our marriage to You. We, Your people, Your bride, were taken from Your torn side, much as Eve was taken from Adam's side. But later we divorced ourselves from You.

Oh, what hatred the soldier must of felt to have speared You after You were already dead! Your blood was shed.

Through all that You hung naked before them without any protection, completely vulnerable before the whole world. Your robe was torn, and sin was now Your covering. Adam hid, but You were exposed! The fullness of the flesh was exposed! You did all of that so we might receive the fullness of who You originally created us to be on earth. As it is in heaven. Right now!

Your blood was shed.

Her God

I died so that you might be recreated into My image, My one. My fullness is for You. Take all of Me, all of My life, for it is available to you. Only believe! See My goodness and love. Keep your eyes on Me and let nothing diminish what has been given to you.

The Girl

Yes, Lord, but that is the difficult part. It is those evil thoughts that come, those deceptive little lies, the negativity that darkness uses to blind us and lead us away.

Her God

My one, hear truth. My word says evil thoughts and such proceed from the heart of man. Judge your heart. Come to Me and confess these thoughts as sin and I will cleanse and purify your heart. So many are blaming the enemy for all those evil thoughts, while taking no responsibility for what is in their heart. Listen to your heart, so you will repent and I will purify it. You must ask Me, then guard your heart and mind. See My way: simple truth.

The Girl

Yes, Lord, we do not like to look in the mirror. It's always easier to blame someone else.

Her God

My perfect love is now in you. Only believe. What is on that mountaintop anyway?

The Girl

The mountaintop where You told me I am supposed to live? Perfect love, living in Your spirit, abiding in You, and You in me—these are what's there. On my mountaintop You are in the Father and the Father is in You, and we are one in each other.

Her God

My one, do not shy away in false humility, stand face-to-face as a friend of God. My one, come with Me closer and focus your eyes on Me. In the narrowness of your scope, see My eyes. The rivers of life that flow endlessly with love are in My eyes. My one, see

My heart as it beats for the tears of a wounded soul. Yes, many continue to walk the path of destruction, not knowing their vision is dulled and blinded to truth, accustomed to deception. As I walk you up this mountain to high places, you will understand love in its fullness, love manifested in action. Do you see?

The Girl

My Lord, I am trying to understand Your love without holding on to a need to protect myself.

Her God

I must work in your inner being, a work that takes much time and a work you do not see until the harvest time when fruit is made manifest.

The Girl

Lord, the will is so strong, isn't it?

Her God

I said I had the power to lay down My life and to pick it up again? My Father gave Me this authority and you have been given it too.

The Girl

We do just that. We lay it down and we pick it up again, we lay it down and we pick it up again.

Her God

It is not accomplished by human might or power, but rather it is done through My Spirit. The will works for whomever is its master, and since the fall it has been working for the flesh—with few exceptions.

The Girl

You are much stronger than our will, right? We were born learning to trust in ourselves. Now You tell us to change everything we know and trust in You. We try, but go back to what we are used to.

Her God

Mercy and grace are My strong foundations laid at the cross for you.

The Girl

As I relearn how to see and live, I will learn to believe in You. Until then I must depend on Your mercy and grace.

Her God

Will you lay down you life for me? The majority have fallen, becoming stuck in ditches dug with their words. They spend their strength seeking to please mankind and long for mankind's acceptance. My foolish ones give themselves over to this pathway of pain and tears. My one, when will you see? Trust Me, and trust My Word. In simplicity of heart, trust Me, for you will be held accountable for every idle word.

The Girl

I am sorry, Lord. Help me so I will not justify my actions and take You for granted in ignorance of Your truth.

Her God

Ignorance is no excuse, My one. I love you.

The Girl

I love You.

I Love You

Do you have shame hiding in your heart? Tell the Lord about it in the spaces below.

_____

_____

_____

_____

_____

_____

_____

_____

_____

_____

_____

_____

_____

_____

_____

_____

_____

_____

_____

Do you want to live free from shame? If so, let God speak to you about how you can live in the beauty of nakedness (innocence), which is created in purity. Write down what He says to you.

_____

_____

_____

_____

_____

_____

_____

_____

_____

_____

_____

_____

_____

_____

_____

_____

_____

He experienced the power of sin in its fullness, the shame and fear, to provide a cover for you to be free. Tell Him what you feel about His sacrifice on your behalf.

_____

_____

_____

_____

_____

_____

_____

_____

Think of instances in which your love was selfish, but you thought it was God's pure love. Tell God about those times and how your love falls short.

_____

_____

_____

_____

_____

_____

_____

_____

_____

Ask Him to reveal His love to you. Write about your experience.

_____

_____

_____

_____

_____

_____

_____

_____

_____

_____

_____

_____

_____

_____

_____

_____

_____

_____

_____

_____

And he will love thee, and bless thee, and multiply thee: he will also bless thee. Deuteronomy 7:13

What is on the mountaintop God is calling you to? Ask Him to show you where He is taking you.

_____

_____

_____

_____

Do you live face-to-face as a friend of God? Ask God to let you live with Him as His close and beloved friend. Write down His answer.

_____

_____

_____

_____

_____

_____

_____

_____

_____

_____

_____

_____

_____

_____

_____

_____

_____

_____

_____

Coming Soon:

FITS, MISFITS, AND COUNTERFEITS
The Body of Christ
A cry to return to the garden!

Send letters for speaking requests to:

Teri Copley
13351D Riverside Dr. #513
Sherman Oaks, CA 91423
sonsetministries.org or tericopley3@aol.com

Additional copies of this book and other book titles from DESTINY IMAGE are available at your local bookstore.

For a complete list of our titles, visit us at www.destinyimage.com Send a request for a catalog to:

Destiny Image₍₎ Publishers, Inc.

P.O. Box 310
Shippensburg, PA 17257-0310

"Speaking to the Purposes of God for This Generation and for the Generations to Come"